Habitats

Mountains

Andrea Rivera   j 577.53 RIV

abdopublishing.com

Published by Abdo Zoom, a division of ABDO, PO Box 398166, Minneapolis, Minnesota 55439. Copyright © 2018 by Abdo Consulting Group, Inc. International copyrights reserved in all countries. No part of this book may be reproduced in any form without written permission from the publisher. Launch!™ is a trademark and logo of Abdo Zoom.

Printed in the United States of America, North Mankato, Minnesota.

092017

012018

THIS BOOK CONTAINS RECYCLED MATERIALS

Photo Credits: iStock, Shutterstock

Production Contributors: Kenny Abdo, Jennie Forsberg, Grace Hansen, John Hansen

Design Contributors: Dorothy Toth, Neil Klinepier

Publisher's Cataloging-in-Publication Data

Names: Rivera, Andrea, author.

Title: Mountains / by Andrea Rivera.

Description: Minneapolis, Minnesota: Abdo Zoom, 2018. | Series: Habitats | Includes online resource and index.

Identifiers: LCCN 2017939223 | ISBN 9781532120688 (lib.bdg.) | ISBN 9781532121807 (ebook) | ISBN 9781532122361 (Read-to-Me ebook)

Subjects: LCSH: Mountains--Juvenile literature. | Biomes--Juvenile literature. | Habitats--Juvenile literature.

Classification: DDC 577.5--dc23

LC record available at https://lccn.loc.gov/2017939223

Table of Contents

Science...4

Technology 12

Engineering 14

Art.. 16

Math.. 18

Key Stats................................ 20

Glossary................................. 22

Online Resources..................... 23

Index 24

Science

Mountains are tall, steep land masses.

They are all over the world.

Trees, grasses, and flowers can grow on mountains. But some are covered in snow all year long.

Many mountains have a **timberline**. Shrubs, mosses, and grasses can grow above it.

Animals live on mountains.

Only certain animals live above the **timberline**. Mountain goats, yaks, and snow leopards are examples.

Animals, like gorillas and giant pandas, live below the **timberline**. They can move and find food more easily.

Technology

Mountains get a lot of rain and snow. The water fills streams and rivers. Some of this water flows through **power plants**.

Engineering

Skiing is a popular sport! Gondolas are small cars that carry skiers up mountains.

Art

Mount Rushmore is in South Dakota. This giant **sculpture** was completed in 1941.

It is the faces of four United States presidents.

Math

Mauna Kea is the tallest mountain. Its total height is 33,500 feet (10,210 m). But most of its height is under water.

Mount Everest is 29,035 feet (8,849 m) above sea level. It has the highest **altitude**.

- The highest known mountain in our solar system is Olympus Mons. It is on Mars. It is 69,459 feet (21,171 m) tall.

- Mountains can be found in oceans.

- The world's longest mountain range is in the Atlantic Ocean. It is called the Mid-Atlantic Ridge. The mountain peaks rise above the water and form islands.

Glossary

altitude – the height of a thing above earth or above sea level.

power plant – a group of buildings, machinery, and equipment where electrical power is generated from another energy source, such as moving water.

sculpture – an object made by carving, chiseling, or molding.

timberline – the land elevation beyond which trees will not grow due to lack of water and oxygen.

Online Resources

For more information on mountains, please visit **abdobooklinks.com**

Learn even more with the Abdo Zoom STEAM database. Visit **abdozoom.com** today!

Index

animals 8, 9, 10

gondola 14, 15

Mauna Kea 18

Mount Everest 19

Mount Rushmore 16, 17

plants 6

power plant 12

rain 12

rivers 12

ski 14

snow 6, 12

South Dakota 16

streams 12

timberline 7, 9, 10